CW01431884

"What's in a name? That which we call a rose by any other name would smell as sweet"
- William Shakespeare, *Romeo & Juliet*

Within the context of Verona's star-crossed lovers, Juliet may have been onto something when telling Romeo that their surnames shouldn't keep them apart, but picking your baby's name is one of the first of many important decisions you'll make for them in life - and the pressure to choose something good can feel huge!

In this guide you'll find gorgeous and unusual name options grouped by theme. There are colour-in star options for two people to choose their favourites and a summary space at the end of each theme section. Why not colour in your star below, with what you would like to be known as to your new bundle of joy?

☆ Known as:_____

☆ Known as:_____

Also included is access to a spreadsheet showing the Top 100 Names in England and Wales since 1996, so you can see if your favourite names are popular. Where a Top 100 name appears in this book, it is noted. The sheet is updated yearly so you can always check it for the most up to date figures. Head to https://rb.gy/bvl7tm or scan the QR code below.

I hope this book inspires some naming magic and even if you don't choose a name contained within these pages, have fun exploring the countless options to gift your child with. Happy naming!

Contents

A note on genders

We have marked next to a name whether it is traditionally M/F/N (male/female/gender neutral) but of course, language is constantly evolving and so are names. Names that traditionally would have only been male like Noah are now in use in female and gender-neutral forms, sometimes with a slight spelling change (for example, Noa). You choose the name that works for your child best.

VINTAGE

Alma (F)
Latin origin, meaning "nurturing soul"

Audrey (F)
English origin, meaning "noble strength"
See also FILM & TV – Audrey Hepburn; MUSICALS – the heroine and killer plant in *Little Shop of Horrors* and SHAKESPEARE – country girl who marries Touchstone in *As You Like It*

August (M)
German origin, meaning "great", "magnificent"

Betty (F)
Hebrew and English origin, meaning "oath of God"

Brooks (M)
English origin, meaning "of the brook"

Cecilia (F)
Italian origin, meaning "hidden"
See also MUSIC – Saint Cecilia is the patron saint of music

Clyde (M)
Scottish origin, meaning "river"
See also NATURE – the River Clyde flows through Glasgow

Dale (N)
Old English origin, meaning "valley"
See also DISNEY – the cheeky chipmunk Dale and MUSICALS – Dale Tremont from *Top Hat*

Della (F)
German origin, meaning "noble"

Earl (M)
English origin, meaning "warrior", "nobleman"

Etta (F)
German, French and English origin, meaning "home ruler"
See also MUSIC - Etta James

Floyd (M)
Welsh origin, meaning "grey haired"
See also MUSIC – Pink Floyd

Frank (M)
German, English and French origin, meaning "free", "Frenchman"

Georgiana (F)
Greek origin, meaning "farmer"
Pronounced two ways:
George-ee-ah-na or George-ay-na

Griffin (M)
Welsh origin, meaning "strong lord"

Herbie (M)
German and Old English origin, meaning "illustrious warrior"

Ida (F)
Greek and German origin, meaning "prosperous", "hard-working"

Ilene (F)
Irish origin, meaning "strength", "little bird"

Joss (N)
English and German origin, meaning "champion", "the merry one"

Laurie (N)
Latin origin, meaning "symbol of victory"
See also MUSICALS – Laurey (F) is the romantic lead in *Oklahoma* and LITERATURE - Laurie (M) is the March sister's neighbour in *Little Women*

Leslie/Lesley (N)
Scottish origin, meaning "garden of holly"
Leslie is traditionally the male spelling and Lesley the female spelling

Matthias (M)
Hebrew origin, meaning "gift of god"

☆ ☆

Milo (M)
Latin and Old German origin, meaning "soldier", "merciful"
Appears in the Top 100 for male births: 87 (2022), 83 (2021), 80 (2020)

☆ ☆

Myrtle (F)
Latin origin, meaning "evergreen shrub"
See also NATURE – myrtle is used as an herbal remedy to treat respiratory ailments and soothe skin inflammation

☆ ☆

Nell (F)
English origin, meaning "bright", "shining one"
See also SHAKESPEARE – the first name of Mistress Quickly in *Henry IV Part 2*

☆ ☆

Otto (M)
German origin, meaning "wealth"

☆ ☆

Percy (M)
French origin, meaning "one who pierces the valley"

☆ ☆

Rufus (M)
Latin origin, meaning "red head"

☆ ☆

Sidney (N)
Old English origin, meaning "island in a river" ☆ ☆

Vera (F)
Russian origin, meaning "faith" ☆ ☆

Our top VINTAGE names:

☆ _____

☆ _____

☆ _____

DISNEY

Adella (F)
Old German origin, meaning "noble"
One of Ariel's sisters in *The Little Mermaid*

Andrina (F)
Greek origin, meaning "brave"
One of Ariel's sisters in *The Little Mermaid*

Bambi (F)
Italian origin, meaning "child", "baby girl"
Bambi is a young male deer, but the name tends to be a feminine choice

Bert (M)
Initially a nickname of German origin, meaning "bright", "noble"
The lovable chimney sweep from *Mary Poppins*, a cute nickname for Robert and Albert

Buzz (M)
Old Norse and American origin, meaning "village in the woods"
Toy Story's Buzz Lightyear was named for astronaut Buzz Aldrin, one of the original men on the moon

Elias (M)
Hebrew and Greek origins, meaning "the Lord is my God"
Walt Disney's middle name
Appears in the Top 100 for male births: 96 (2022)

Esmeralda (F)
Spanish and Portuguese origin,
meaning "emerald"
The heroine of *The Hunchback of Notre Dame*, based
on the Victor Hugo novel (see also LITERATURE)

Evangeline (F)
Greek origin, meaning "bearer of
good news"
The evening star, whom the firefly Ray is in love with, in
The Princess and the Frog

Flora (F)
Latin origin, meaning "flower"
One of Sleeping Beauty/Aurora's
three good fairy godmothers
See also GODS & GODDESSES – Roman fertility
goddess of flowers and springtime

Flynn (M)
Irish origin, meaning "descendant
or son of Flann"
Flynn Rider is the chosen name of Rapunzel's
smouldering companion in *Tangled*, real name: Eugene
Fitzherbert

Giselle (F)
French and German origin,
meaning "pledge"
The princess who lands in modern day New York in
Enchanted

Gus (M)
Latin origin, meaning "majestic",
"exalted"
One of Cinderella's cute mouse friends

Maui (M/N)
Hawaiian and Māori origin,
Trickster god
The trickster god in *Moana*, also the second biggest island in Hawaii
See also GODS & GODDESSES

Mickey (M)
Hebrew origin, meaning "who resembles God"
The legendary Mickey Mouse, who narrowly missed out on being called Mortimer thanks to Walt Disney's wife Lillian

Minnie (F)
Originally a nickname for names of German and Hebrew origin,
meaning "of the sea" and "protection"
Fashionista and classic Disney character, Minnie Mouse
See also MUSIC – 1931 Cab Calloway song "Minnie the Moocher"

Nora (F)
Latin origin, meaning "honour",
"shining light"
One of the main characters in *Pete's Dragon*

Raya (F)
Hebrew and Arabic origin meaning
"friend", "queen"
The Guardian of the Dragon Gem in *Raya and the Last Dragon*, uniting the tribes and breaking the Druun curse which turns everyone to stone

Sullivan (M)
Irish origin, meaning "black-eyed one"
Sully is the employee of the month, every month in *Monsters Inc*

Walter (M)
Old High German origin, meaning "commander of the army"
Of course, the name of the inimitable Walt Disney

Woody (M)
American origin, meaning "from the lane in the woods"
Toy Story's big hearted cowboy Woody

Our top DISNEY names:

_____

_____

_____

MUSICALS

Adelaide (F)
Old High German origin, meaning "noble natured"
In *Guys and Dolls*, the long-suffering cabaret singer Miss Adelaide has been engaged to Nathan for 14 long years but eventually gets her way
See also DISNEY - *The Aristocats*

Albin (M)
Latin origin, meaning "white", "bright"
If done right, Albin's Act 1 ending anthem, "I Am What I Am", is an incredible moment in *La Cage Aux Folles*

Audra (F)
Old English, French and Lithuanian origin meaning "noble strength", "storm"
The legend that is Audra McDonald. Winner of six Tony Awards - more than any other actor and in all four acting categories
See also VINTAGE

Barnaby (M)
Old English origin, meaning "son of consolation"
Barnaby Tucker is the young assistant to Cornelius Hackl in *Hello, Dolly!*
See also VINTAGE

Billy/Billie (N)
Old High German origin, meaning "resolute protector"
Billy Bigelow is *Carousel*'s loveable rogue
Appears in the Top 100 for male births: 98 (2008), 89 (2007) 82 (2006), 71 (2005, 2004, 1999 &1996), 84 (2003), 81 (2002), 78 (2001), 76 (2000), 68 (1998), 70 (1997)

Bobby/Bobbie (N)
German origin, meaning "bright", "fame"
Bobby (or Bobbie in the latest version) is the central role in Stephen Sondheim's *Company*, a perpetual singleton who discovers that maybe love and commitment aren't so bad after all
Appears in the Top 100 for male births: 80 (2022), 73 (2021 & 2018), 70 (2020), 68 (2019), 65 (2017), 90 (2016), 67 (2015), 71 (2014), 59 (2013), 57 (2012), 76 (2011), 83 (2010)

Chess (N)
Latin origin, from Chester (M) meaning "camp of soldiers" and German origin, from Francesca (F) meaning "Frenchman"
The non-ABBA musical written by Benny Anderson and Bjorn Ulvaeus with Tim Rice

Effie (F)
Gaelic origin, meaning "well spoken"
Effie White is the full-figured lead singer of The Dreamettes, the band at the heart of *Dreamgirls*
See also FILM & TV – one of the leading characters on teen drama *Skins*

Evan (N) ☆ ☆
Welsh origin, meaning "God is gracious", "youth"
Dear Evan Hansen, from Benj Pasek and Justin Paul, was a huge success on Broadway for both the writers and leading actor Ben Platt
Appears in the Top 100 for male births: 83 (2013), 86 (2012), 82 (2011), 76 (2010), 70 (2009), 80 (2008), 81 (2007), 85 (2006), 97 (2005), 99 (2004)

Idina (F) ☆ ☆
English origin, meaning "prosperous friend"
Tony Award winner Idina Menzel (or Adele Dazeem as we're talking about names!), the original Elphaba in *Wicked* and voice of Elsa in DISNEY'S *Frozen*. Named for her great-grandmother, Ida
See also DISNEY

Irene (F) ☆ ☆
Greek origin, meaning "peace"
Irene opened on Broadway in 1919 and ran for 675 performances, at the time the longest-running musical in Broadway history and a record unbeaten for nearly two decades

Mabel (F) ☆ ☆
Latin origin, meaning "lovable"
The nobody-turned-somebody heroine in Jerry Herman's *Mack and Mabel*
Appears in the Top 100 for female births: 50 (2022), 58 (2021), 68 (2020), 98 (2019)

Orin (M)
Hebrew origin, meaning "pine tree"

He might be Audrey's sadistic dentist boyfriend in *Little Shop of Horrors* but ignoring that, this is a super cute boy's name
See also NATURE – a sweet yellow apple from Japan

Pippin (N)
German origin, meaning "awe inspiring"

The fantastical story of magic and (extra)ordinary life by Stephen Schwartz
See also LITERATURE and FILM & TV – Pippin was one of Frodo Baggins' friends who left the Shire to join the Fellowship of the Ring

Sutton (N)
English origin, meaning "from the southern homestead"

Tony Award winner Sutton Foster got her big break in *Thoroughly Modern Millie*, after the original leading lady left nine days before the show opened

Sweeney (N)
Irish and Gaelic origin, meaning "small hero"

Yes, I am serious about including the mass murdering barber Sweeney Todd. A Sondheim anti-hero is the perfect namesake for your little bundle of joy. Just maybe steer them clear of a career in barbering or hairdressing...

Usnavi (M)
American origin, meaning "US Navy"
A book about names and a musical theatre section wouldn't be complete without Usnavi from *In The Heights*, whose immigrant parents named him after a US Navy ship they saw on their way into America

Our top MUSICALS names:

MYTHS & LEGENDS

Albion (M)
Latin origin, meaning "white land"
One of the earliest recorded
names for Great Britain, a reference to the White Cliffs
of Dover

☆ ☆

Ajax (M)
Greek origin, meaning "eagle"
A hero of the Trojan War as told in
Homer's *Iliad*, renowned for his large stature and
bravery

☆ ☆

Arjun (M)
*Sanskrit origin, meaning
"lustrous", "made of silver"*
A legendary archer in the *Mahabharata*
See also NATURE – Arjun tree

☆ ☆

Circe (F)
Greek origin, meaning "bird"
A Greek sorceress who turned
men into pigs (and back again – maybe they deserved it
at the time!)

☆ ☆

Cressida (F)
Greek origin, meaning "golden"
Cressida was a Trojan woman
whose father defected to the Greek side in the Trojan
war
See also SHAKESPEARE – from *Troilus and Cressida*

☆ ☆

Cyrus (M)
Persian and Greek origin, meaning "sun"
Cyrus was a Persian King in the *Iliad*

Embla (F)
Scandinavian origin, meaning "elm"
In Norse mythology, Embla is one of the first human beings

Evander (M)
Greek and Scottish origin, meaning "good man", "bow warrior"
In Greek Mythology, Evander was an early King of Arcadia

Fae (F)
French origin, meaning "fairy"
A gorgeous, unusual spelling for your little fairy

Hector (M)
Greek origin, meaning "steadfast", "to hold"
In Greek mythology, Hector was a hero of the Trojan War revered for his bravery and honour. Also the name of the knight who raised King Arthur
See also SHAKESPEARE – appears in *Troilus and Cressida*

Isolde (F)
Welsh, German and Celtic origin, meaning "fairy lady"
The Arthurian legend of *Tristan and Isolde* describes the tragic love story between an Irish princess and Cornish knight

Lancelot (M)
English origin, meaning "servant", "God-like"
Sir Lancelot was King Arthur's closest friend and ally (he did also steal his wife but let's leave that out!). A family name in this author's Mansfield mining family in the 19th century

Leda (F)
Greek origin, meaning "woman", "happy"
Leda was the Queen of Sparta in Greek mythology, a woman of great beauty. Just don't ask her about geese

Lorelai (F)
German origin, meaning "alluring enchantress"
A maiden turned siren in German folklore, luring men to their deaths with her song around the rocky headland of the Rhine
See also FILM & TV – the first name of both *The Gilmore Girls*

Marian (F)
Hebrew origin, meaning "rebellious", "star of the sea"
Maid Marian was Robin Hood's better half in English folklore, an early feminist icon

Megara (F)
Greek origin, meaning "great", "pearl"
The wife of Heracles in Greek mythology
See also DISNEY – the damsel in distress who can handle it in the animated *Hercules*

Merlin (M)
Welsh origin, meaning "sea fortress"
King Arthur's legendary mentor and magician

Owain (M)
Welsh and Greek origin, meaning "youth", "well born"
The 6th century Welsh historical Owain became incorporated into Arthurian legend, where he is also known as Ywain, Yvain, Ewain or Uwain
See also LITERATURE – *Yvain, the Knight of the Lion* and *Owain, or the Lady of the Fountain*

Phoenix (N)
Latin origin, meaning "legendary bird"
A phoenix is a mythical bird that when its life reaches an end, emerges born again from the ashes of its own funeral pyre

Pixie (F)
Celtic origin, meaning "fairy"
A gorgeous ethereal name, pixies are said to be from Cornwall and Devon

Rune (N)
Old Norse origin, meaning "secret"
Runic alphabets are native to the
Ancient Germanic peoples: runes can be used to
represent concepts in addition to sound values

Tristan (M)
Welsh origin, meaning "sorrowful"
One of the Knights of the Round
Table and the tragic hero of *Tristan and Isolde*

Our top MYTHS & LEGENDS names:

GODS & GODDESSES

Aganjú (M)
Yoruba origin
Warrior King

☆ ☆

Aker (M)
Egyptian origin
God of the Earth and the horizon

☆ ☆

Aine (F)
Celtic origin
Goddess of wealth and summer

☆ ☆

Athena (F)
Greek origin
Goddess of wisdom and warfare

☆ ☆

Atlas (M/N)
Greek origin
Atlas holds the Earth and heavens
on his shoulders, a punishment for rebellion against
Zeus

☆ ☆

Dalia (F)
Lithuanian origin
Goddess of destiny
See also NATURE – Dahlia flowers

☆ ☆

Diana (F)
Roman origin
Goddess of hunting and the moon
See also FILM & TV – Diana is the real-world name of
DC's Wonder Woman and SHAKESPEARE – Diana
appears in *All's Well That Ends Well*

☆ ☆

Iris (F)
Greek origin
Goddess of the rainbow
See also NATURE – perennial flower
Appears in the Top 100 for female births: 66 (2022), 70 (2021), 77 (2020), 81 (2019 & 2017), 82 (2018), 84 (2016)

Izanami (F)
Japanese origin
Goddess of creation

Jumala (M/N)
Finnish origin
Sky God

Juno (F)
Roman origin
Queen of the Gods, goddess of marriage and childbirth
See also FILM & TV – eponymous 2007 Indie film

Juri (M)
Estonian origin
God of agriculture

Kana (N)
Hawaiian and Japanese origin
A Maui demigod who could take the form of a rope and stretch from Molokai to Hawaii

Kengue (M)
Kongo origin
The Sky Father and primordial creator of all life

Loki (M)
Norse origin
Norse trickster god of mischief

☆ ☆

Maeve (F)
Irish origin
Goddess of love and desire
Appears in the Top 100 for female births: 48 (2022), 77 (2021), 94 (2020)

☆ ☆

Odin (M)
Norse origin
Norse god of both war and death

☆ ☆

Sabrina (F)
Celtic origin
River goddess
See also FILM & TV – *Sabrina the Teenage Witch*, classic 90s/00s teen sitcom

☆ ☆

Zeus (M)
Greek origin
Zeus defeated the Titans to become king of the Gods on Mount Olympus

☆ ☆

Our top GODS & GODDESSES names:

☆ _____

☆ _____

☆ _____

FILM & TV

Adaline (F)
German origin, meaning "nobility"
From the 2015 film, *The Age of Adaline*, where the title character who stops ageing is played by Blake Lively

Arwen (F)
Welsh origin, meaning "noble maiden"
An Elvish princess in JRR Tolkien's *Lord of the Rings*
See also LITERATURE for the namesake books

Buddy (M)
English origin, meaning "friend"
Buddy the Elf from *Elf*
See also MUSIC – Buddy Holly

Casper (M)
Persian origin, meaning "treasure bearer"
A cute and friendly ghost
See also RELIGIOUS – Caspar was one of the Three Wise Men at the Nativity

Clementine (F)
French and Latin origin, meaning "mild", "merciful"
Clementine is a 1985 French/Japanese animated television series about the fantastic adventure of 10-year-old Clementine Dumat, who is a wheelchair user. A cult classic in Europe

Elodie (F)

French origin, meaning "foreign riches"

The princess who saves herself in 2024 film, *Damsel*, played by Millie Bobby Brown

Appears in the Top 100 for female births: 73 (2022), 93 (2021), 96 (2020)

Lux (N)

Latin origin, meaning "light"

Kirsten Dunst's character in *The Virgin Suicides*

See also GAMING - the Lady of Luminosity in the *League of Legends* games

Maverick (M)

English origin, meaning "independent"

The nickname of Tom Cruise's character, Lieutenant Pete Mitchell, in the 1986 film *Top Gun*

Neo (M)

Latin and Tswana origin, meaning "new", " gift"

The leading role in *The Matrix* series

Nola (F)

Gaelic origin, meaning "white shoulder"

The heroines of Spike Lee's *She's Gotta Have It* and Woody Allen's *Match Point*

Ripley (N)
Old English origin, meaning "meadow"
Ellen Ripley is the original hero of the *Alien* franchise
See also LITERATURE – Patricia Highsmith's *The Talented Mr Ripley*

Rocky (M)
English, German and Italian origin, meaning "rock", "rest"
Rocky Balboa, the boxer who made Sylvester Stallone a household name
See also NATURE

Truly (F)
English origin, meaning "honestly"
Truly Scrumptious, *Chitty Chitty Bang Bang's* leading lady
See also MUSICALS for the stage version of the same name

Valerian (M)
Latin origin, meaning "strong", "healthy"
In HBO's *Game of Thrones*, Valyria was a once-great ancient civilisation, famed for its use of dragons in war and expensive Valyrian Steel. Valerian was also the name of a 3rd century Roman Emperor
See also LITERATURE for George RR Martin's *Game of Thrones* books

Vesper (F)
Latin origin, meaning "evening star"
Vesper Lynd, the conflicted anti-hero in James Bond film *Casino Royale* (2006)

Yvaine (F)
Scottish origin, meaning "evening star"
The literal fallen star played by Claire Danes in the Neil Gaiman novel and movie *Stardust* (see also LITERATURE)

Our top FILM & TV names:

☆ _____

☆ _____

☆ _____

NATURE

Aspen (N)
American origin, meaning "quaking tree"
☆ ☆

Avon (N)
Celtic origin, meaning "river"
The river Avon runs through the middle of England and is the main waterway running through William Shakespeare's hometown, Stratford-upon-Avon
☆ ☆

Basil (M)
Greek origin, meaning "royal", "kingly"
See also VINTAGE
☆ ☆

Bear (M)
German origin, meaning "bear"
☆ ☆

Blossom (F)
British origin, meaning "flower like"
☆ ☆

Bran (M)
Scottish and Irish origin, meaning "bramble", "raven"
See also LITERATURE and FILM & TV - George RR Martin's Bran Stark
See also GODS & GODDESSES – Celtic god of the underworld
☆ ☆

Corbin (M)
British origin, meaning "crow"
See also FILM & TV and MUSICALS
– Corbin Bleu, Broadway performer and one of the actors in the *High School Musical* film series

Eden (N)
Hebrew origin, meaning "paradise"
See also RELIGIOUS - the Garden of Eden was the original paradise on Earth
Appears in the Top 100 for female births: 87 (2022), 91 (2021), 98 (2020)

Emerald (F)
Greek origin, meaning "green gemstone"
See also FILM & TV – Emerald Fennell is an Oscar Award winning actress and director

Fern (F)
Old English origin, meaning "one who lies among the ferns"

Forrest (M)
French, British and Latin origin, meaning "woodland"

Hazel (F)
English origin, meaning "the hazelnut tree"

Iona (F)
Scottish origin
A small island off the coast of Scotland

Jasper (M)
Hebrew and Persian origin,
meaning "treasurer", "gemstone"
A gemstone – cryptocrystalline quartz to be exact
Appears in the Top 100 for male births: 78 (2022 &
2020), 79 (2021), 84 (2019), 89 (2018), 98 (2016)

Juniper (F)
Latin origin, meaning "young"
A small evergreen shrub

Onyx (N)
Greek origin, meaning "claw",
"nail"
Onyx is a strong, hard gemstone. Also a Pokémon

Peony (F)
Greek and Latin origin, meaning
"praise giving", "healing"
Peonies are a beautiful sought-after flower, in season
for only a few months a year

Quillan (M)
Irish origin, meaning "cub"

River (N)
English origin, meaning "flowing
freely"
See also FILM & TV – actor River Phoenix and River
Song, the Gallifreyan name of Doctor Who's time-
travelling wife

Robin/Robyn (N)
Greek origin, meaning "famed", "bright"
A bird, often linked with Christmas
See also MYTHS & LEGENDS – Robin Hood; FILM & TV – Batman's sidekick, Robin and SHAKESPEARE – the tailor-turned-actor in A *Midsummer Night's Dream*
Appears in the Top 100 for female births: 71 (2022 & 2021), 74 (2020), 65 (2019), 72 (2018), 79 (2017), 86 (2016), 84 (2015), 100 (2014)

Sage (N)
Latin origin, meaning "wise"
A tasty green herb

Sylvan (M)
Latin origin, meaning "of the forest"

Violet (F)
English and Latin origin, meaning "purple"
Sweet violet is a perennial with beautiful purple flowers
Appears in the Top 100 for female births: 43 (2022), 45 (2021), 48 (2020), 51(2019), 53 (2018), 62 (2017), 65 (2016), 68 (2015), 71 (2014), 78 (2013), 100 (2012)

Wade (M)
English and Scandinavian origin, meaning "to go", "ford"
A sea-giant of Germanic folklore (see also MYTHS & LEGENDS)
See also FILM & TV – Wade Wilson aka Deadpool

Wren (N)
English origin, meaning "little bird"
A songbird

☆ ☆

Our top NATURE names:

☆ _____

☆ _____

☆ _____

LITERATURE

Arrietty (F)
British origin, meaning "dainty", "gorgeous"
Arrietty is one of the tiny Borrowers, who live below a clock

Atticus (M)
Latin origin, meaning "from Attica", "rugged coast"
The protagonist of Harper Lee's Pulitzer Prize-winning *To Kill A Mockingbird*

Beatrix (F)
Latin origin, meaning "voyager"
Beatrix Potter is a writer and illustrator best known for her children's books featuring characters such as Peter Rabbit, Jemima Puddleduck and Jeremy Fisher. A sweeter version of Harry Potter's Bellatrix

Bennett (N)
Latin origin, meaning "blessed", "well spoken"
For any Mr Darcy lovers, the five Bennet sisters from Jane Austen's *Pride and Prejudice* provide inspiration for this traditionally masculine but now more gender-neutral name, commonly spelled Bennett

Caspian (M)
Latin origin, meaning "white"
The hero of CS Lewis' *Chronicles of Narnia*, Prince Caspian

Cordelia (F)
Latin and Celtic origin, meaning "daughter of the sea"
King Lear's one nice daughter (see also SHAKESPEARE)
See also FILM & TV – character in *Buffy the Vampire Slayer*

Ender (M)
Turkish origin, meaning "rare"
Ender's Game is a 1985 military science fiction novel by American author Orson Scott Card
See also FILM & TV for the film of the same name

Enola (F)
Native American origin, meaning "solitary"
The sister of Sherlock, Enola Holmes is a detective in her own right

Finnick (M)
British and Scottish origin, meaning "marshland", "water meadow", "dwelling place"
Finnick is a previous champion of *The Hunger Games*, doing everything he can to keep his true love, Annie, safe

Heath (M)
English origin, meaning "land of heather and grass"
A name inspired by Emily Bronte's *Wuthering Heights* and the brooding Heathcliff
See also FILM & TV – the brilliant actor Heath Ledger

Hester (F)
Persian origin, meaning "star"
The plain arctic hare daemon of
Lee Scoresby in the *His Dark Materials* series by Philip
Pullman

Lennox (N)
Scottish and Gaelic origin,
meaning "elm grove"
The Secret Garden's heroine Mary Lennox discovers an
abandoned garden on her uncle's estate
See also NATURE – the elm tree and SHAKESPEARE – a
thane in *Macbeth*

Minerva (F)
Latin origin, meaning "the mind"
The stern but fair head of
Gryffindor House in the *Harry Potter* series
See also GODS & GODDESSES – Roman Goddess of
crafts and wisdom

Nancy (F)
Middle English origin, meaning
"grace", "favoured"
The original teenage detective, Nancy Drew
Appears in the Top 100 for female births: 65 (2021), 66
(2020), 64 (2019 & 2018), 67 (2022 & 2017), 70 (2016),
71 (2015), 90 (2014)

Roald (M)
German and Norse origin, meaning
"fame"
Writer Roald Dahl created some of the best-known
children's books in the world, including *Matilda, The*
Witches and *Charlie and the Chocolate Factory*

Sawyer (N)
English origin, meaning
"woodcutter"
Made famous by Mark Twain's *The Adventures of Tom Sawyer*

Our top LITERATURE names:

_____

_____

_____

MUSIC

Allegra (F)
Italian origin, meaning "joyful", "lively"
Inspired by the musical term allegro, meaning "at a brisk speed"

Bowie (N)
Scottish origin, meaning "yellow-haired"
The music icon David Bowie, master of multiple identities and rebranding

Cadence (F)
Latin origin, meaning "falling"
The end of a phrase in which the melody or harmony creates a sense of full or partial resolution

Cole (M)
English origin, meaning "charcoal"
From the music legends Nat King Cole and Cole Porter

Jarvis (M)
French origin, meaning "servant spear"
British musician Jarvis Cocker became a figurehead of the Britpop genre with his band Pulp
See also FILM & TV – Tony Stark's AI who later becomes the Marvel superhero Vision

Jazz (N)
American origin, meaning "spirit",
"lively"
The word "jazz" came to mean jazz music in Chicago around 1915

Jude (N)
Latin origin, meaning "praised"
"Hey Jude" by The Beatles
Appears in the Top 100 for male births: 32 (2022), 40 (2021), 53 (2020), 47 (2019), 56 (2018), 50 (2017), 62 (2016), 61 (2015), 65 (2014), 72 (2013), 71 (2012), 83 (2011), 86 (2010), 98 (2009)

Lennon (N)
Gaelic origin, meaning "blackbird",
"lover"
The legendary John Lennon lends his name to this beautiful neutral choice

Lyric (F)
French and Greek origin, meaning
"words set to music"
"Lyrics" i.e. "words set to music" was first attested in Stainer and Barrett's 1876 Dictionary of Musical Terms

Mack (M)
Scottish and Irish origin, meaning
"child of the handsome one"
Kurt Weill and Bertolt Brecht's song written for the music drama *The Threepenny Opera*, "Mack the Knife"
See also MUSICALS – *Mack and Mabel*

Melody (F)
Greek origin, meaning "song"
A melody is the main tune in music
See also DISNEY – Ariel's daughter in *The Little Mermaid 2: Return to the Sea*

Nash (M)
Middle English origin, meaning "at the ash tree"
A gorgeous name if you are a fan of country music and its home of Nashville, Tennessee

Viola (F)
Latin origin, meaning "violet"
A string instrument, slightly larger than a violin with a deeper sound
See also SHAKESPEARE – Shakespeare's heroine in *Twelfth Night* and NATURE – edible purple and yellow flowers

Ziggy (N)
German origin, meaning "victorious protector"
One of David Bowie's alter egos, Ziggy Stardust

Our top MUSIC names:

☆ _____

☆ _____

☆ _____

RELIGIOUS

Amari (N)
Hebrew, Sanskrit and Latin origin, meaning "goddess", "promised by God"

Amos (M)
Hebrew origin, meaning "carried by God"
One of the twelve minor prophets in the Bible/Torah

Asher (M)
Hebrew origin, meaning "happy one", "fortunate", "blessed"
One of Jacob's twelve sons

Delilah (F)
Hebrew origin, meaning "delicate"
Delilah was Samson's wife who gave him a much-needed haircut. Which also destroyed all his strength, thus betraying him
See also MUSIC – "Hey There Delilah" by the Plain White T's and not forgetting Tom Jones
Appears in the Top 100 for female births: 44 (2022), 50 (2021), 62 (2020), 76 (2019), 90 (2018)

Ezra (M)
Hebrew origin, meaning "help"
Appears in the Top 100 for male births: 46 (2022), 51 (2021), 59 (2020 & 2018), 60 (2019), 81 (2017), 91 (2016)

Ira (N)
Hebrew origin, meaning "watchful"
One of David's heroes
See also VINTAGE

Iscah (F)
Hebrew origin, meaning "to behold"
The niece of Abraham in The Book of Genesis. Believed to be the source name for "Jessica"

Jonah (M)
Hebrew origin, meaning "dove"
A prophet swallowed by a whale

Jyoti (F)
Sanskrit origin, meaning "light", "radiance"
A Hindu goddess of light

Keziah (F)
Hebrew origin, meaning "sweet-scented spice", "cinnamon bark"
A daughter of Job

Levi (M)
Hebrew origin, meaning "joined", "attached"
Third son of Leah and Jacob

Nevaeh (F)
American origin, meaning "heaven"
Heaven spelled backwards!

Rudra (N)
Sanskrit origin, meaning "one who drives away evil"
A divine archer in Hinduism and the father of the storm gods

Samson (M)
Hebrew origin, meaning "sun"
Appears in the Bible and Torah as the last of the judges of the Israelites
See also SHAKESPEARE – as Sampson, opens *Romeo and Juliet* with Gregory

Zayan (M)
Arabic origin, meaning "radiant", "handsome", "nice"
From Urdu Muslim culture

Our top RELIGIOUS names:

_____

_____

_____

GAMING

Astarion (M)
Greek origin, meaning "little star"
Astarion is an elf with roguish
charms in *Baldur's Gate 3*

Drake (M)
*English origin, meaning "dragon",
"snake"*
Nathan Drake is the gentleman explorer from
Unchartered
See also NATURE – a male duck is called a drake

Kitana (F)
Lebanese origin, meaning "light"
A fierce warrior princess in the
Mortal Kombat series

Link (M)
English origin, meaning "ring"
Link is the protagonist in the
Legend of Zelda games

Peach (F)
British origin, meaning "fruit"
Mario's beloved Princess in the
Nintendo game series

Sonic (M)
Latin origin, meaning "sound"
Sonic might be a blue hedgehog
from another world, but it is a super cute name

Zelda (F)

German origin, meaning "grey fighting maid"

Zelda is the eponymous Princess in the *Legend of Zelda* games. The brilliant actor Robin Williams named his daughter Zelda after this character

See also FILM & TV – Sabrina's aunt in *Sabrina the Teenage Witch*

Our top GAMING names:

RANDOM

Amo (M)
*French origin, meaning "little
eagle"*

☆ ☆

Asa (N)
Hebrew origin, meaning "healer"
*Swedish origin, from an ancient
Norse name meaning "gods" (pronounced "o-sa")*
Yoruba origin, meaning "hawk" (pronounced "asha")
Igbo origin, meaning "beautiful" (pronounced "aa-saa")
Japanese origin, meaning "morning"
*Indonesian, Nepali, Punjabi and Filipino origin,
meaning "hope"*
A beautiful name with lots of meanings across different
cultures

☆ ☆

Aubin (M)
*French origin, meaning "white",
"bright"*

☆ ☆

Aurelie (F)
Latin origin, meaning "golden"
This beautiful French sounding
name is perfect if you love the more popular Aurora and
Ottilie but still want something unique

☆ ☆

Bleu (N)
French origin, meaning "blue"

☆ ☆

January (F)
*Latin origin, meaning "month of
Janus"*

☆ ☆

Lane (N)
English origin, meaning "a small roadway or path"

☆ ☆

Manon (F)
French and Welsh origin, meaning "wished-for-child", "star of the sea", "beautiful Queen"

☆ ☆

Noelle (F)
French origin, meaning "Christmas"

☆ ☆

Nye (N)
Welsh origin, from Aneurin (M) meaning "man of honour"
Aneurin Bevan, who as Minister for Health, was instrumental in setting up the National Health Service

☆ ☆

Paloma (F)
Latin origin, meaning "dove"

☆ ☆

Sonny (M)
British origin, meaning "son"

☆ ☆

Willem (M)
Dutch origin, meaning "resolute protector"
Willem was a contestant on the 4th series of *RuPaul's Drag Race* in 2012

☆ ☆

Yukina (F)
Japanese origin, meaning "fortune", "endure"

☆ ☆

Zachkiel (M)
English origin meaning "gift of God"

☆ ☆

Our top RANDOM names:

☆ _____

☆ _____

☆ _____

SHAKESPEARE

Adriana (F)
Latin origin, meaning "from Hadria"
Adriana in *The Comedy of Errors* is a proto-feminist distraught that her husband is paying attention to another woman and irritated that men are not as bound as women are, nor women as free as men

Albany (M)
Latin origin, meaning "of Alba"
The Duke of Albany is Goneril's husband in *King Lear*, greedy for her father's kingdom

Aragon (M)
Spanish origin, meaning "high valley"
The Prince of Arragon is an unsuccessful suitor to Portia in the *Merchant of Venice* and Katherine of Aragon appears in *Henry VIII*
See also LITERATURE and FILM & TV for a similar sounding name to *The Lord of the Rings'* Aragorn

Ariel (N)
Hebrew origin, meaning "lion of God"
The spirit bound to Prospero in *The Tempest*
See also DISNEY – the human-loving mermaid Ariel

Cade (N)
English origin, meaning "round", "barrel"
From John Cade who leads a proletarian rebellion in *Henry VI, Part 2*

Ferdinand (M)
German origin, meaning "bold voyager"
The only son of the King of Naples in *The Tempest*. A very cute nickname would be Ferdie

Grey (N)
British origin, meaning "grey coloured"
Appears in *Richard III* as one of the sons of Queen Elizabeth and *Henry V* as one of the conspirators against the king
See also LITERATURE – the spicy novel with multiple variations of colour, *50 Shades of Grey*

Hamnet (M)
Old German and French origin, meaning "home"
The name of Shakespeare's only and much-loved son, possibly linked to *Hamlet*

Hermia (F)
Greek origin, meaning "messenger"
Described by Helena in *A Midsummer Night's Dream* as "though she be but little, she is fierce!"

Hero (F)
Greek origin, meaning "hero", "brave defender"
Hero is in love with Claudio in *Much Ado About Nothing*. Falsely accused of adultery, she fakes her death
See also FILM & TV – Hiro (M) must save the cheerleader to save the world on *Heroes*

Jupiter (N)
Latin origin, meaning "god of the sky"
Hears the pleas of the ghosts of Posthumus' family in *Cymbeline*
See also GODS & GODDESSES – the supreme deity of the Roman gods

Mariana (F)
Portuguese origin, meaning "star of the sea"
Appears in both *Measure for Measure,* bed swapping with Isabella, and in *All's Well That Ends Well* as Helena's childhood friend

Ophelia (F)
Greek origin, meaning "help", "advantage"
The tragic heroine in *Hamlet*
Appears in the Top 100 for female births: 81 (2022)

Orlando (M)
Latin origin, meaning "sound"
The hero and lover in *As You Like It*
See also FILM & TV – Orlando Bloom

Portia (F)
Latin origin, meaning "pig" (a much prettier name than its namesake!
Portia disguises herself as a lawyer in *The Merchant of Venice* to try and save Antonio's life

Regan (N)
Irish origin, meaning "little king",
"sovereign"
One of *King Lear*'s daughters. Your Regan will hopefully treat you nicer than this Regan treats her father

Rosaline (F)
German origin, meaning "soft
horse", "beautiful rose"
Appears in both *Romeo and Juliet* as Romeo's prior love and as a quick witted, intelligent woman in *Love's Labour's Lost*

Sebastian (M)
Greek origin, meaning
"venerable", "revered"
Viola's brother in *Twelfth Night* and also appears in *The Tempest* as Alonso's younger brother
See also DISNEY – the crab who keeps an eye on curious mermaid Ariel
Appears in the Top 100 for male births: 39 (2022, 2020), 38 (2021, 2014, 2013), 34 (2019), 28 (2018), 35 (2017, 2015), 36 (2016), 41 (2012), 47 (2011), 58 (2010), 62 (2009), 77 (2008), 87 (2007), 94 (2006), 89 (2005), 90 (2004), 88 (2003), 96 (2002)

Thaisa (F)
Greek origin, meaning "beloved",
"bandage"
Believed dead in *Pericles, Prince of Tyre*, she becomes a priestess at the temple of Diana

Valentine (N)
Latin origin, meaning "strong", "healthy"

A much-loved name by Shakespeare, appearing in *The Two Gentlemen of Verona, Twelfth Night, Titus Andronicus* and *Romeo and Juliet*

See also RELIGIOUS – a Roman 3rd century Saint

Our top SHAKESPEARE names:

_____

_____

_____

GRATITUDE AND ACKNOWLEDGEMENTS

There are multiple thanks owed, but the two most important are:

To everyone who proof-read and gave me such great feedback, thank you so much. Your advice and support was and is, much appreciated.

To my family and friends for always supporting my crazy ideas and finally to my husband and our little one – I keep your names in my heart always.

Printed in Great Britain
by Amazon

46046564R00036